Wounded Soul

N. NIAMI

Published by: N. Niami

For information contact:
N. Niami
www.nniami.com

First Printing, 2021
ISBN: 978-0-6489327-8-9 (paperback)

Wounded souls are the most beautiful souls on this planet. Wounded souls have experienced pain like no other. But they didn't let what they've been through hardened their heart. On the contrary, it softened their heart, and they are the most gracious, loving, and compassionate souls you will ever encounter. We've all suffered and experienced things we wish we didn't need to experience. Yet the experiences we all go through either make us or break us. The choice is ours.

Your soul may be wounded but it's not broken. Your spirit may be weary but it's not crushed. Don't give up on your wounded soul because your will wounds heal in time and they will turn into the most beautiful beauty marks. Your brokenness will turn into greatness and your greatest lessons will turn into your greatest blessings.

Noor Nianni

To be strong is to be vulnerable and to
be vulnerable is beautiful.

N. Niami

Dedicated to you
Let go of what is hurting your heart and soul
because you deserve peace, joy, and freedom.

This is my intention for you
and for the world.

Wounded Soul

Love didn't break you.
Loving the wrong person
broke you. It was giving your
heart to someone who was not
worthy of it.

You gave them your all and
they knew it. You put them
first and they loved it. They
promised you the world and
you fell for it. They tore you
down and you broke for it.
But they also gave you the
opportunity to rebuild a more
beautiful life than the life you
had with them.

Wounded Soul

Though you knew it was going
to happen and though you saw
it coming, it still hurt because
you didn't want to do the one
thing you were so afraid of
doing; break your heart by
letting them go. Yet it was
your last option to save what
was left of your soul.

Loving them was the worst
form of self-destruction and
self-sabotage. You ended up
breaking your own heart by
loving them. You sabotaged
your own self to take care of
them. In the end you emptied
yourself out of everything good
trying to fill them yet nothing
was able to fill the black hole
within them.

Wounded Soul

The sad part is they get used
to mistreating you because in
the end they knew you'll
always be there waiting for
them and giving them another
chance. They were right but
only until it was their last
chance because you finally
chose to walk away and never
look back again.

How long are you going to
wait for something you know
may never happen? How much
longer are you going to put
your life on hold for someone
who may never be ready? Let
them go because you deserve
someone who is ready to be
with you wholeheartedly and
not someone who is unsure of
their love for you.

Wounded Soul

They have hurt you more than
you deserved because you have
trusted them more than they
deserved. But hold your head
up high because you were
someone they didn't deserve
and in time they will see that
they have lost the best thing
that's ever happened to them.

Stop going back to the person
your heart is trying to heal
from. The person who broke
your heart cannot be the one
to mend it. Only you can heal
your heart and it starts by
letting that person go.

Wounded Soul

At first, you may be in denial
about losing them to protect
yourself from the pain. But do
you know what's going to hurt
you more? Seeing how they
didn't fight to keep you when
all you've been doing is
fighting not to lose them.

I hope you know that you
deserve it all. You deserve the
best life has to give you. You
deserve to be happy and free.
You deserve to be loved and
seen. You deserve to not only
be loved by others but also by
yourself. You deserve all the
love you freely give to others.
You deserve the world and
everything in. Never forget
that.

Wounded Soul

You were madly in love with
them that you ignored how
poorly they treated you and
how miserable they made you
feel. Now you know that it is
better to be alone than to be
with someone who makes you
question your worth of being
loved. It's better to be alone
and happy than to be
miserable with somebody.

You don't find your worth and
value in someone else. You
find your worth and value
within yourself and then you
find a person who is worthy of
being with you. Remember
that.

Wounded Soul

You'll never know how
damaged someone is until you
try to love them in hope for
your love to heal them. But
then you realise you broke
yourself in an attempt of
fixing them because the more
you tried to love them the
more they tried to hurt. It's
not your responsibility to fix
people and you can't help
those who don't want to be
helped.

They thought you were always
going to be there and they
were right; you were. You were
always there for them and
they took that for granted. But
they were wrong to think you
were going to be there forever.
And just like that they woke
up one day and you were gone.
Last chances don't usually
come with warnings.

Wounded Soul

You may have taken a while to
let them go but that's only
because you were still waiting
and hoping for the impossible
to happen. That maybe one
day they will see your worth
and fight to be with you. That
maybe one day they tell you
they loved you and couldn't be
without you. It was a day that
never came to be.

They were the reason you
smiled but they were also the
reason you cried. They were
the source to your happiness
but also the source to your
sadness. The only person who
can make you feel better is
the same person who is
making you feel worse.

Wounded Soul

If I decided to give up on you,
you need to understand that it
was the hardest thing for me
to do. I'm the sort of person
who sees the best in people
and stayed with you even
when everyone was telling me
to leave you. So if I decided to
give up on you then be sure
that it took everything in me
to leave you because I also left
a part of me with you, a part
I'll never have back.

I don't know why I was so
afraid of losing you as though
you were mine. Truth is you
were never mine to begin with
and you cannot lose someone
who was never yours.

Wounded Soul

You gave so much of you to
them. You gave up your all
until you had nothing else to
give. You gave your best but
even your best wasn't enough
for them. So sometimes you
have to forget how you feel
and remember what you
deserve.

You will be amazed at what life
has to offer you once you start
believing in yourself and in
what you deserve. Sometimes
you need to let go of what you
think you want so that you can
receive what you truly deserve.

Wounded Soul

You were a lover with a big heart. You refused to give up on people especially those who meant something to you. You chose to see the best in everyone. It was until you were broken down so many times, you had no choice but to give up on those who broke your heart and let go of those who tore your soul apart.

Don't be sorry for giving them
so much love. They will be
sorry for not wanting any of it.
They will look for your love in
everyone else but they won't
find it because your love
wasn't just an ordinary love.
Your love was one of a kind. It
was an extraordinary love.

Wounded Soul

Little did you know the one
you loved the most was going
to be the one to hurt you the
most. You gave them so much
love and in exchange they
gave you so much pain. They
walked away feeling too good
for you and you walked away
feeling not enough.

Yes it was hard giving up on
everything you wanted. But it
was going to be harder waiting
for something you knew
wasn't going to happened.
You shouldn't be with someone
who needs to think twice
about being with you. You
deserve someone who wants to
be with you as much as you
want to be with them.

Wounded Soul

Never lose hope. No matter
how dark everything is now it
won't always be this way.
After every storm comes a
rainbow and after every rainy
day comes sunshine. Don't
lose hope, your hard work will
pay off soon and you will be so
glad you never gave up but
pushed through till the end.

Don't question why someone
keeps hurting you. The
question you should be asking
is why you keep letting them
hurt you. Don't let your love
for them turn you into slavery.
If they keep hurting you is
because you keep letting
them. Forgiving someone
doesn't mean you give them
another chance to disappoint
you with.

Wounded Soul

I want you to know one thing;
just because I let you go
doesn't mean I ever wanted to.
In fact, I didn't walk away;
you pushed me away. I tried
everything so that we could
remain together and you tried
everything to tear us apart.

They cheated because they
wanted to. They lied because
they wanted to. And the only
reason why they were sorry is
because they got caught. It's
always about them and never
at all about how they made
you feel. Remember that next
time you want to forgive them
and let them back in your life.

Wounded Soul

Sometimes you just have to
ask yourself how many times
someone you love has to hurt
you before you finally face the
truth. Someone who loves you
wouldn't hurt you and someone
who hurts you doesn't love you.

The most heartbreaking
moment is when you say
goodbye to someone you
thought you were going to
spend the rest of your life
with. Saying goodbye to what
you thought was going to be
your forever.

Wounded Soul

You knew it was over but you
also knew it never really
began. You were so afraid of
losing them but then you
realised they didn't care about
losing you. Your only fear was
having to let them go. And
when you did what you feared
the most, you had nothing else
to fear. So in losing them you
were finally free.

They wanted you but only
when it suited them. They
loved you but only when they
wanted someone to love.
They missed you but only
when they were alone.
They only wanted you when
they needed you but they were
never there for you when you
needed them. Walk away from
one sided love because you'll
continue to be the one giving
and getting nothing in return.

Wounded Soul

The thing about loving
someone with all your heart is
that you will always have a
place in your heart for them.
But a place in your heart
doesn't mean a place in your
life. You can still love them
but not need them in your life.
You can still miss them and
not want them back.

You walked away still loving
them and wanting to be with
them. You walked away still
hoping it was going to be them.
You walked away wishing they
would hold on to you the way
you had held on to them. You
walked away when all you
wanted was to stay.

Wounded Soul

You miss them yes, but you
don't miss who they are. You
miss the person you thought
they were. You miss the
person you made them out to
be. And in both cases that's
not who they are now.

N. Niami

Every time I thought of you,
I would remind myself that if
you wanted to be with me, you
would have. I stopped making
excuses for your lack of action.
You had a choice to fight for us
and you didn't. You gave me no
reason to stay and every reason
to walk away.

Wounded Soul

You love them but you don't
need them. You miss them
but you're better off without
them. You care about them
but you started caring about
yourself too. At one stage you
needed them but now you are
in need of no one but yourself.
In losing them you had found
yourself.

You didn't get your happy
ending with them. Maybe your
happy ending is with you, on
your own. Letting go of
everyone and everything that
is hurting your heart and soul.
Leaving the broken pieces of
yesterday behind and starting
over again. Maybe the happy
ending you're looking for is
between you and yourself.

Wounded Soul

You didn't lie to save me, you
lied to save yourself. You
weren't protecting me from
the truth; you were stopping
me from finding out the truth.
Your lies weren't to protect
me, you lied to protect
yourself. So never again tell me
you lied to protect me because
nothing hurt me more than
finding out you lied to me.

If you are constantly trying to
prove your worth to someone,
then maybe it is you who has
forgotten your worth. You
should't have to prove to
anyone that you are worthy.
Know your worth even if they
don't and stand in your truth
no matter what.

Wounded Soul

Wanting to go back to the
same person who hurt you is
a big mistake. But a bigger
mistake is thinking that it's
going to be different this time
around. It'll only be the same
or worse.

You will never be good enough
for the wrong person. No
matter what you do for them
it'll never be enough. But for
the right person you will be
more than enough. Don't let
the wrong person ruin your
chances of being with the
right one.

Wounded Soul

The best way to avoid
disappointment is to not
expect anything from anyone.
And the way to stop expecting
anything from anyone is to
start giving yourself what you
need others to give you. You
have everything you need
inside of you, you just have to
dig deep to get to it.

Stay away from people who can't take responsibility for their actions and toxic behaviour. From people who make you feel bad for being angry at them when they do wrong. There comes a time to stop trying to make things right with the wrong people because no matter what you do it'll never be enough and it will always be your fault.

Wounded Soul

Walk away from people who
are not willing to climb to the
top with you. Walk away from
situations that steal away your
peace. Walk away from those
who are trying to hold you
back and put you down. The
more you walk away from
what no longer serves you
the happier you will become.

Forgiveness doesn't excuse
their actions. Forgiveness
isn't giving them another
free pass. Forgiveness stops
their actions from destroying
your heart and sets you free
from the pain. So you can
forgive someone and not allow
them back in your life again.

Wounded Soul

A person who values you
wouldn't put themselves in a
position to lose you. If they
choose to lose you and walk
away be sure to let them.
Don't force or beg anyone to
stay in your life. If they want
to leave, escort them to the
door and trust that whoever
is meant to be there will still
be there.

If you weren't there when I
needed you the most, what
makes you think I'll ever need
you again? If you weren't with
me when life was hard what
makes you think you'll be
with me when life is great?

Wounded Soul

You can rise up from anything
no matter how hard the fall
was. You can overcome
everything and you will.
Nothing is permanent. You're
not stuck, this isn't the end,
you're not giving up. You have
choices. Decide to move
forward and never look back.
The hardest choices we make
turn out to be the best choices
we've ever made. You got this.

This is the woman who would
have done anything for you.
She gave up on herself just to
be with you. She gave up on
all her dreams to help you
fulfill yours. But you were
silly enough to lose a woman
like her and look at you now,
searching for her in everyone
you meet but she won't be
found.

Wounded Soul

They may have knocked you
down lower than you've ever
been to but they also gave you
the chance to rise higher that
you ever were. Those who hurt
you have also unknowingly
helped you and blessed you by
awakening you to the true
power you hold from within.

N. Niami

When you find yourself
constantly treating a person a
lot better than they treat you.
It's time to realise that no
matter how good you are to
someone it's not going to
make them a better person.
You can't love someone into
loving you no matter how
much you love them. Just let
them be and you go on about
your way in peace.

Wounded Soul

Letting go of anything you
held close to your heart is one
of the hardest things you'll do
in life. Letting go is going to
be the hardest decision you
make but it will also turn
into the best decision you
made. When you believe you
deserve better letting go
becomes a lot easier.

And one day she was done
with it all. She was done with
putting herself last. She was
done letting people take her
for granted. She was done
denying her own feelings.
She was done with loving the
wrong people and started
loving herself. Because she
realised she was far more
worthy of her own love than
anybody else.

Wounded Soul

If you hesitate to make a
decision about choosing me.
Let me make it easier for you
by taking myself out of the
equation. Don't choose me
because the minute I became
an option for you was the
minute you lost me.

I have forgiven you not
because you deserved
forgiveness but because I
deserved peace and freedom.
My act of forgiveness had
nothing to do with you.
Forgiveness was freeing
myself from the pain you
caused me and taking back
the power I had given you.

Wounded Soul

You are scared to let go
because you believe you will
be in so much pain. But the
pain you're in today is
because of your refusal to let
go. You're in pain because you
are choosing to hold onto
something that is hurting you.
It's time for you to let go and
set yourself free.

Closure happens the moment
you accept things for what
they are and not try to control
or change the outcome.
Closure comes with acceptance
and letting go of the illusion of
what should've been. Accept
things as they are and have
faith in what will be because
one day you will look back and
understand why things had to
happen the way they did.

Wounded Soul

We don't always need a plan
and we don't always need to
have all the answers.
Sometimes we just need to
breathe, let go, trust, and see
what happens. Have faith that
everything will work itself out
and you will live a far more
beautiful and fulfilling life
than the one you had hoped
for before.

No one has the right to judge
you. No one has the right to
tell you how to live your life.
No one has the right to tell
you how you should feel. Not
unless they've lived your life,
walked your path, suffered
your pain, fought your battles
and go through what you've
been through. Live your life
unapologetically because you
don't owe anyone anything.

Wounded Soul

You can't change someone
who doesn't see an issue in
their actions but you can stop
their actions from hurting
you. Don't waste your time
and energy on people who
refuse to take accountability
for their poor behaviour. The
only way to win with a toxic
person is not to play at all.

Don't allow someone who betrayed you make you feel it was your fault. It was never your responsibility to teach them how to grow up and act like adults. Some people act like little kids yet they want you to treat them like an adult.

Wounded Soul

They didn't poison you
overnight; they poisoned your
soul slowly, little by little. So
don't expect the poison to
leave you all at once. It will
leave you little by little and
you will cleanse your soul from
the pain. This is your healing,
be patient, loving, and kind to
yourself.

N. Niami

You never know how strong
you really are until someone
you love tries to break you.
Then you will know that you
are unbreakable. You may
stumble and fall but you will
never break because one has
the power to crush your spirit.

Wounded Soul

When someone has to decide
between choosing you or
someone else, help them
make their decision by
walking away. You are not
someone's option or backup
plan, and don't be someone's
second choice. Let it be that
either choose you or lose you.
And if they lose you then they
never really deserved you.

N. Niami

Don't let the person who
didn't love you make you
believe you are unlovable.
Their inability to love you
doesn't define your worthiness
of being loved. Just because
they didn't love you doesn't
mean that you can't be with
someone who will love you
beyond anything you've ever
felt before.

Wounded Soul

A woman becomes a reflection
of how you treat her. If you
don't like how she's acting up
then maybe take a good look
at how you are treating her.
Don't be the devil and expect
to be with an angel. Angels
don't live in hell.

You owe yourself the biggest
apology for trying to settle for
less than what you deserve.
You put up with people
mistreating you, people who
didn't deserve your time and
effort. You placed their needs
before your own. Make
yourself a promise that the
love you will have for others
will never be greater than the
love you have for yourself.

Wounded Soul

They gave you every reason to
walk away but you didn't.
You loved them more than
they could ever love you.
A part of you hoped that
someday they will love you
and fight to be with you. But
then you realised you were
waiting for something that
was never going to happen.

You emptied yourself out of
your own love just so that
they could love you back.
But maybe it wasn't their love
you were after, maybe the love
you needed is your own love
for yourself. Yet you kept
withholding it to give to
someone else.

Wounded Soul

If God didn't give you what you
wanted, it's because He has
something better for you. What
you want is not always what
you need. And if one door
closes, a bigger one will open.
Trust and have faith that what
is coming is going to be so
much better than anything
you've left behind.

When you heal, you will
understand why you went
through what you've been
through. Everything will make
sense and you will understand
why you had to break because
it was in your brokenness you
found your true strength.

Wounded Soul

And one day you will wake up
and they won't be the first
thing you think about. You
don't care about what they're
up to or who they're with. You
will accept they are only a part
of your past but have no place
in your future. This is all part
of letting go and moving on.

Nothing takes more courage
than starting over again after
your world has been shattered
and scattered into pieces.
Nothing takes more strength
than rebuilding yourself again
after you've been broken.
Whenever you feel like giving
up, take a look at how far
you've come and all the things
you've overcome.

Wounded Soul

Strength grows when you do
the things you thought you
couldn't do. At one stage you
couldn't picture life without
them but now, you can't
picture life with them.
The person you are today is a
lot stronger than the person
you once were and as you
change, your taste in people
changes too.

You are strong because you
have been weak. You are
happy because you have been
sad. You are wiser because you
have made mistakes. Regret
nothing because everything
has shaped you into the person
you are today.

Wounded Soul

Wounds don't heal in time,
it's what you do in time that
will either heal you or make
you a prisoner of your pain.
Healing yourself will be your
greatest responsibility and the
most rewarding and liberating
journey you could embark. Be
courageous enough to take the
road less traveled.

Avoid people who mess with
your peace. People who love
drama and chaos. Your peace
if far more valuable than
being right. Choose your
battles wisely and walk away
from anything that threatens
to steal your peace.

Wounded Soul

Whatever you do, do not go
back to what God had to rescue
you from. Remember how you
couldn't walk away by your
own strength and you needed
the power and grace of God to
get you out of there. God didn't
get you back on your feet so
you could run back to what he
saved you from.

There is nothing more
empowering than forgiving
those who have hurt you and
moving on. Because you trust
that eventually everyone gets
what they deserve. You don't
seek revenge because you
know the best revenge is to
move on and live a happy life.

Wounded Soul

Don't let their words blind you
from seeing their actions.
Actions will always speak
louder than words. Stop
denying the truth because it
makes you feel uncomfortable.
How they treat you will tell
you how they feel about you.

Be courageous enough to teach
yourself to live with their
absence than having to adjust
your boundaries to live with
their disrespect. There's no
reason to tolerate disrespect,
not even love.

Wounded Soul

Decide today to put yourself
first and make yourself a
priority in your life. It's not
selfish to put your needs first,
in fact it's necessary because
you can only take care of
others when you are taken
care of first. Take care of
yourself because you can't
pour from an empty cup.

You gave them many chances
to disappointment you with. So
maybe it's time to make this
their last chance. You can't
put your life on hold until
they change because some
people are incapable of
changing. You can't change
someone who doesn't see an
issue with their actions.

Wounded Soul

Life is too short to worry or
stress about things that are out
of your control. Enjoy the
journey, forget the destination,
regret nothing, and appreciate
everything. Believe that
something amazing is about to
happen in your life and it will.

Be thankful for all those
difficult people in your life.
They were the pressure you
needed to become a diamond
in the making.

Wounded Soul

Don't change yourself for the
sake of pleasing others. You
can't please everybody and
nothing you do will ever be
enough for those people you
are trying to please. Change
yourself only if it pleases you
otherwise be yourself and the
right people will love you for
who you are without wanting
to change you.

You never really knew me to
know what was happening
inside of me. If you knew me
and looked closely into my
soul, you would have seen a
hurting heart and behind my
smile I was falling apart.

Wounded Soul

You always thought they were too good for you. But have you ever thought that maybe the opposite might be true? When you thought you weren't good enough the truth was that you were too good for people like them.

You have the power to choose
what to accept and what to
let go of. Let go of those who
drain you and choose people
who empower you and bring
out the best in you. As you
begin to learn how to love
yourself you will make
healthier decisions leading
you to happier outcomes.

Wounded Soul

If someone continuously hurts
you more than they love you, it
won't matter how much you love
them you'll never be happy
loving someone who's making
you feel miserable.

The heart that's not meant to
love you will leave you. But the
heart that's meant to love you
will fight for you and keep
you. Be patient to wait for
what you deserve and don't
settle for anything less just
because everyone else is.

Wounded Soul

In case you forgot let me
remind you of how worthy
and special you are. You are
worthy beyond measure.
There is only one you and
that's your power. You are
imperfectly perfect with all
your flaws and imperfections.
You are a beautiful
masterpiece in the making.
Don't let anyone tell you
otherwise.

You think you need someone
to complete you as though you
are incomplete. But you are
whole and complete from the
beginning of time. You are a
wonderful masterpiece created
with beauty and love. Whoever
you find will be an addition to
you not a completion of you
because you need not to add
anything to yourself to
experience your true power
and greatness.

Wounded Soul

Your soul may be wounded but it is not broken. Your spirit may be weary but it is not crushed. Sometimes it takes a bad experience and a painful heartbreak to shake us and awaken us into who we really are and what we really deserve.

Sometimes the pain we
experience is too deep to
express. So we sit in silence
and everybody thinks we have
it all together when in reality
every piece of us is falling
apart. You reach a point in
time where you are numb and
have no desire to express your
pain to anyone because no one
will understand what you are
going through but you.

Wounded Soul

You deserve someone who will
love you and treat you like
royalty. You deserve the kind
of love that supports you and
brings out the best in you. You
deserve someone who loves
spending every moment of
their time with you because
they can't picture life without
you. You deserve someone who
makes you feel that you are
seen, valued and loved. That's
the sort of someone you
deserve.

Both of you were unhappy but
neither of you wanted to admit
it. So you kept breaking each
other and called it love. You
kept fighting over everything
yet you thought it was making
you stronger. You denied the
truth about your relationship
and believed in an illusion
because in the end lies don't
end a relationship, the truth
does.

Wounded Soul

Sometimes relationships end
not because it was someone's
fault but simply because it
just wasn't meant to be. You
both tried, you gave it your
best and you worked really
hard to make it happen but it
just wasn't happening. It was
just a relationship that wasn't
meant to be. It's a simple as
that.

It hurts to let go of someone
you love but it hurts more to
hold on to the one who is
constantly hurting you. It hurts
to let go but it hurts more to
hold on because somewhere
deep within yourself you know
you deserve better than this.

The definition of insanity is loving someone who is hurting you and causing you so much pain. Worse yet believing the one who is hurting actually loves you.

Don't fall in love but rise in
love. You shouldn't fall in
love with one another, you
must rise in love with each
other. Falling in love is
dangerous; rising in love is
ecstatic. Don't fall for anyone
but rise to a place of love,
loyalty, and respect.

I didn't leave you just because
you let me down this time. I
left because you let me down
every time I let you back in my
life. And I didn't walk away
because you made a mistake
once but because you kept
making the same mistake
again and again. Making a
mistake once is on you; letting
you make it twice is on me.

What do you do when the only
person who can stop your pain
is exactly the one causing it?

Sometimes, the only reason
you can't let go is because you
are scared of the unknown. So
you rather settle for who you
know even if they're no good
to you. Don't let fear stop you
from pursuing what you truly
want. No power can stand in
your way once you've made up
your mind that you deserve
better.

You loved them even though
they gave you no reason to.
They couldn't love you even
though you gave them a
thousand reason to. This
should tell you that no matter
what you do, you'll never be
good enough for the wrong
person.

Wounded Soul

One of the hardest things you
will ever have to do is mourn
the loss of someone who still
lives in your heart. They're not
with you but they still live
inside of you.

One day they're going to wake
up and notice that they
should've tried because you
were worth the fight. One day
they will look back and realise
they ruined the best thing
that's happened to them. But
when that day comes it'll all
be a little too late.

Wounded Soul

Part of the reason why we
hold onto something so tight
is because we fear that
something good won't happen
twice. But if what you had
was good you wouldn't have
had to leave it in the first
place. Let that sink in.

Never chase anyone. If they
don't want to stay, let them
walk away. The right people
will come into your life and
they will stay. Don't beg
anyone or force anything but
trust that what's meant for
you will never leave you and
that which leaves you wasn't
meant for you.

Wounded Soul

You are worthy of being loved.
You are worthy of being seen.
You are worthy of an effort
and you are worthy of being
somebody's everything. Just
because the last person failed
to see your worth doesn't mean
you can't be with someone who
does. Be patient because great
things take time.

Be with someone who is not
only grateful to have you, but
will also do what it takes to
hold onto you and never lose
you. Because someone who
values you will never put
themselves in a position to
lose you.

Wounded Soul

They weren't in love with
you. They were in love with
how you made them feel.
They didn't miss you, they
just wanted you around when
they needed you. They didn't
want to spend time with you,
they just wanted to be with
you when they were alone.
Do you see the difference?

They expected so much from
you and made you feel nothing
you do is ever enough. You
walked away feeling not
enough. They had a sense of
entitlement and never
appreciated anything you did.
This is because you can't
appreciate something you feel
entitled to.

Wounded Soul

Rejection is for your own
protection. You were saved
from what could've destroyed
you. You may not understand
it now but later you will.
That rejection will serve as a
redirection to something far
bigger and better than what
you wanted for yourself.

Forget them because if they
wanted to be with you, they
would still be here. They would
have found a way to be with
you. But they didn't and no
matter how much you tried,
you couldn't. Let them go
because if you really needed
them and if they really needed
you, you'd still be together.

Wounded Soul

If you never heal from those
who hurt you, you'll start
hurting those who love you.
You didn't have a say in the
pain inflicted on you but you
do have a say in healing
yourself. Don't wait for anyone
to come rescue you because
only you can rescue yourself.

Decide this minute to never
again beg anyone for their
love, attention, time and
effort. Start giving yourself
what you want others to give
you. Then you will realise
everything you needed already
existed within you.

The best apology is changed behaviour. What will an apology serve you if they continue doing the thing they're apologising for? An apology without a changed behaviour is only a form of manipulation not reconciliation.

You don't go around hurting
people in the name of love.
For love doesn't hurt but it
has the power to heal. Love
doesn't break it only builds.
If it didn't do this for you
then it wasn't true love.

Wounded Soul

Beneath everything always
remember that you are a good
hearted person. You have been
hurt over and over again. But
you didn't let that pain make
you heartless. You continue to
love deeply because you refuse
to let anything change the
unfading beauty of your heart.

You can't find security and
safety in something you could
lose. Never depend on
anything or anyone because
they could be here one minute
and gone the next. Depend
only on God for He is your
source to everything. God will
always be there, and unlike
humans, He will never leave
you nor abandon you.

Wounded Soul

Self-love isn't about not loving
them anymore. Self-love is
about realising that the only
love you were ever in need of
was your own love for
yourself. And in order for
others to love you, you must
learn to love yourself because
self-love is the best love you
could ever give yourself.

You can't keep giving
someone the benefit of the
doubt especially if they have
no intention of changing their
behaviour. You need to accept
that some people will not
change because change
requires growth and they have
no intention on growing and
becoming better people.

Wounded Soul

Don't tell me you love me then
show me otherwise. Don't tell
me how much you want to be
with me and find excuses to
keep us apart. Either walk
with me or let me walk away.
I will be fine either way.

Don't be someone's sometime,
when they only want you when
they need you. If they can't be
there for you all the time then
don't waste any of your time
on them. You deserve someone
who makes you a priority, not
an option or a part-time.

Wounded Soul

Someone's actions towards you
is a reflection of their feelings
for you. Don't justify their lack
of effort and tolerate their
behaviour. What you tolerate,
you also encourage. You are
teaching people how to treat
you. Teach them well.

If they are giving you plenty of
reasons to leave stop making
excuses for you to stay. If they
don't appreciate your presence
let them appreciate your
absence. Someone who doesn't
appreciate you surely doesn't
deserve you.

Wounded Soul

At one stage, you lost yourself
trying to hold onto everyone in
your life. Now you're losing
everyone trying to find
yourself. When you find
yourself you will find all the
answers you have been looking
for. The peace you have been
searching for and the
happiness you have been
waiting for. Being lost is also a
part of being found.

Your peace is more valuable
then trying to find all the
answers to understand why
something happened the way
it did. Sometimes you just
need to let go of what was and
have faith in what will be.
Sometimes you just need to
trust the process even when
you don't understand it.

Wounded Soul

Painful endings will lead you
to beautiful beginnings.
Don't worry about the hard
times because the most
beautiful blessings come from
our hardest lessons and
difficult roads always lead to
beautiful destinations.

131

Maybe you don't need to be
with anyone right now. Maybe
this is your chance to get to
know yourself for the very first
time. Maybe this is your sign
to take this time to workout
who you are and what you
stand for. What you want and
who you want to be. All this
time you have been focused on
someone else, maybe now it's
time for you to focus on
yourself. You are worthy of the
time and energy you keep
investing into others.

Wounded Soul

Healing doesn't happen as
quickly as you want it to.
Healing takes time, it's a
process and every process
takes times. Give yourself that
time. Give yourself that grace.
Be kind and loving to yourself
because you are trying to hold
it together when everything in
you is falling apart.

After a very long and hard
time, you just had enough.
You finally accepted that you
couldn't make it happen all on
your own. You had enough of
forcing what's not meant to
be. You had enough and that's
when you decided to let go and
let it be because what's meant
to be will always be.

Wounded Soul

Sometimes what life throws at
you gets a little heavy. And
sometimes you may need to
breakdown and have moment
to put yourself back together.
But throughout all of this
trust that you will be okay in
the end. Everything will be
okay because life has a funny
way of working things out.
You just need to surrender
and let it all go.

When you realise you can do
better because you deserve
better, you will make a
decision to not settle for
anything less than what you
want. It all starts with you and
what you believe you are
worthy of. Believe that you are
worthy of the best, and the
best you shall receive.

Wounded Soul

Instead of wiping away your
painful past, wipe away the
people who made it painful.
Instead of wiping away your
tears, wipe away the people
who made you cry.

N. Niami

Fall in love with someone who
sees the battle scars within
you and still calls you
beautiful. This is the kind of
love you deserve. A love so
pure, it only brings out the
best in you.

Wounded Soul

And when they ask you about
me I hope the truth cuts
through you like a double
edged sword. You broke the
one person whose only
intention was to love you and
be with you forever.

It's better to break your heart
once when you walk away
than to have them break your
heart every single day you are
with them.

Wounded Soul

And maybe we both came in
each other's life for this one
reason. I came into your life to
teach you how to hold on, and
you came into mine to teach
me how to let go.

Your life with the narcissist
was never meant to be. It was
only meant to help you heal
and awaken you to who you
truly are and what you truly
deserve.

Wounded Soul

You can't make someone who
doesn't see an issue with their
actions take responsibility or
admit fault. They don't believe
what they've done is wrong and
tell you you're overreacting.
This is how they get away with
what they've done; by
invalidating how you feel.

You are the sort of person who
cheers everyone up even when
you're hurting from the inside.
You are the sort of person who
continues to give love no
matter how much pain you've
been given. You are the sort of
person who is so rare and
profound. Don't let anything
change the sort of person you
are because you are one of a
kind.

Wounded Soul

In time you will realise the
best thing they have done for
you was refusing to be with
you so you can learn how to be
with yourself and enjoy your
own company.

Whenever you find yourself
missing them, remind yourself
that if they wanted to be with
you nothing could've stopped
them. Remember that next
time you want to give them
another excuse for their lack
of effort.

Become so strong and secure
within yourself to have the
courage to walk away from
anything that isn't bringing
you peace. If it's not bringing
you peace, it's not worth your
time nor your tears.

If they moved on then maybe
it's your turn to do the same.
Holding onto someone who
has already let you go is only
going to hurt you. Do yourself
a favor and set yourself free.
You can choose to be free in
any moment, let this moment
be now.

Wounded Soul

One day you will wake up and
they won't even cross your
mind. You will not miss them
anymore or obsess over them.
You won't even remember how
you felt about them or how
they made you feel. That day
will be one of the best days of
your life because you simply
don't care anymore.

You were doing okay before
you met them. But now you'll
do better after you've met
them. They have shown you
what you don't want and in
return you figured out what
you truly want and will get.

Wounded Soul

You will thank them for
leaving you because they will
put you in the arms of
someone who will be loving
you. A love so deep and
genuine, the sort of love you
were always worthy of. The
sort of love they were
incapable of giving you.

N. Niami

Once you get what you have
been praying for, you will
wonder why you were even
stressing for. Because what
you have prayed for is going to
be worth the wait and you'll
be so glad you never settled for
anything less.

Wounded Soul

Never forget how they made
you feel. This feeling will stop
you from going back to the
person who broke you.

And one day they are going to
miss you and wish they had
never pushed you away. They
are going to realise they
should've fought to keep you
because you were everything
they wanted and everything
they lost.

Wounded Soul

Some days will harder than
others. Some days you will
find yourself missing them
more than usual. Thinking
about them more often and
wanting to be with them at all
cost. And that's okay, because
your love for them was far
more real than their love ever
was for you.

N. Niami

They broke your soul. They
tore your heart apart. They
shattered all your dreams and
abandoned you when you
needed them the most. Think
of this every time you want to
give them another chance to
hurt you with.

Wounded Soul

Don't allow their poor
behaviour to become your
norm. Nothing is worse than
becoming used to the pain
they are inflicting on you and
believing that's what you
deserve. Nobody deserves to
be hurt.

Truth be told; there were
many red flags but we chose
to ignore them and believe in
what we wanted to be real.
The same red flags we ignored
were the reason why we ended
up here.

Wounded Soul

You were everything you
could've been for them. You
were their lover and best
friend. Making them happy
was your priority. So much so
that you forgot about yourself
and your own happiness.
Remember that next time you
blame yourself for the way
things ended.

Your heart still loves them but
your mind is telling you to get
over them. A part of you
wants to be with them and the
other part doesn't. You can't
be with them yet you can't be
without them. This is when a
battle is raging within you. On
one hand you want to be with
them and on the other you
know you should leave them.
And usually the hardest
decision is the right decision
to make.

Wounded Soul

You will break but you will
also heal. You will cry but you
will always smile. You will be
hopeless but you will also be
hopeful. You've been through
bad days but you will also go
through good days. Never lose
hope and always trust that
better days are coming
because the best is yet to be.

N. Niami

Once your heart breaks it'll
never be the same again.
You can try and put the
broken pieces back together
but it'll never look the same.
A heartbreak will change
you in ways you didn't think
is possible.

Wounded Soul

What you have been through
teared you down but it will
also rebuild you. It weakened
you but it will also make you
stronger. Let life make you
stronger, wiser and kinder.
And trust that life is always
working out for you even when
it doesn't look like it.

When you tolerate their bad
behaviour, you are also
encouraging it. You can't
make people treat you better
but you can choose what you
accept into your life. Your
boundaries are there to
protect you so be sure to
protect your peace at all cost.

Wounded Soul

If you have difficulties loving
yourself then you will find it
difficult loving anyone else.
Loving yourself is a daily
commitment you need to make
because how you treat yourself
will be how others treat you.
Treat yourself with love,
kindness, and respect and
everybody else will do the
same. It all starts and ends
with you.

Here's a question for you to
ponder on and answer within
yourself. How much longer are
you willing to stay on this
road, knowing it is going to
end in more heartbreak and
turmoil? How many more signs
do you need to confirm what
you've known all along?

Wounded Soul

If they were quick to walk
away and never look back
then it was because they
never intended to stay in the
first place. If they let you go
so easily then they never held
onto you to begin with. Now
it's your turn to do what
they've done a long time ago.
Let them go and move on.

Letting go is never easy.
Letting go of how you thought
your life would look like with
the person you thought was
'the one' is painful and hard.
No one said it is going to be
easy but it's worth it. As you
begin to let go of the old you
make space for the new and
something better will enter
your life.

Wounded Soul

If they made you cry then
don't think about giving them
another try. Don't let your
heart find ways to forgive
them when all they've done is
hurt the heart that loved them.

Soon you will heal and
overcome the mountain
standing in front of you. You
will let go of everything that's
been weighing you down. You
will move away from everyone
who is trying to hold you back.
Soon you will find your way
back to yourself and move
forward with confidence and
courage to a better place.

Wounded Soul

You'll never know how strong
you really are until being
strong is the only option you
have left.

You were always good enough.
You just gave your best parts to
the wrong people and this
made you believe you were
never good enough. Give your
best parts to the right people
and you will be more than
enough.

Wounded Soul

A good heart in a cold world
happens to suffer the most.
This is why your heart has
been let down more times
than you can remember.
Because a good heart always
loves, always trusts and it
always sees the best in people
who least deserve it.

You have been forcing things
for a quite a while and
nothing has happened. So
then, why don't you let go a
little and see what happens?

Wounded Soul

No matter what you are going
through right now I promise
you that everything will work
out in the end. I don't know
how or when but I know that it
will. Have faith that
everything will fall into place
at the perfect time. You are
not behind and nothing is ever
too late. Life has a funny way
of working things out. Let life
surprise you in the most
beautiful ways.

Hold onto your beautiful heart
and be so proud of it. Your
heart was broken by those it
loved the most, it was
betrayed and played with.
Yet somehow it remained
beautiful, kind, and loving to
this day. A heart so rare to
find these days.

Great relationships only
happen when both people love
each other enough and care
about one another to make it
work. The reason why most
relationships fail is because
one is trying and the other one
isn't and it takes two to tango.
One of you cared too much and
the other didn't care enough.

Life will present you with
choices all the time. Every
situation can make you bitter
or better. Every obstacle can
break you or make you.
Become a victim or the hero
of your own story. The choice
is yours, choose carefully.

Wounded Soul

Some days will harder than
others. In those days you can't
even get yourself out of bed.
You're alive but it's as though
everything inside of you is
dead. You yell out the loudest
silent cry and wonder should
you even give life another try.
But please remember things
will get better no matter how
dark it may be right now. Even
after the worst storms, the sun
will shine again and your
darkest days will lead you into
your brightest days.

Nothing is permanent and
nothing remains as is. Where
you are right now is not final
and the pain you're going
through is not permanent.
Never lose hope. This too
shall pass.

Wounded Soul

She gave you more than you
deserved and she loved you
more than you can ever love
her but in the end you didn't
appreciate what she had to
offer. So she decided to walk
away and never look back
because she knew that she
deserved someone better
than you.

N. Niami

In the end you will overcome
everything you once thought
you couldn't. What you didn't
have the strength to do back
then you have done with
courage. Strength doesn't
come from what we can do,
but it comes from doing the
things we thought we
couldn't do.

Wounded Soul

You justified their poor
behaviour and gave them
excuses for the way they
treated you because a part of
you didn't want to believe that
you loved the wrong person. A
part of you didn't want to
believe they're not who you
thought they were.

You made the mistake
everyone else makes. You
equated your self-worth with
their inability to love you.
Their inability to love you
doesn't mean you are
unlovable. It simply means
they are incapable of loving
you or anyone else. It says
nothing about you but
everything about them.

Wounded Soul

And despite everything you've
been through and how people
have treated you. You will
always be worthy and loved by
the right people. One bad
chapter in your life isn't the
end of your story. Don't give
up until you get to your
happily ever after.

Shine in front of those who
thought you couldn't. Don't let
anyone dim your light for no
light shines brighter than the
light that comes from within.
Your light will irritate the
darkness in them and that, is
not your problem.

Wounded Soul

Stop worrying and doubting
because it will not change a
single thing. Only being
hopeful and faithful can
change everything. Remember
both faith and fear require
you to believe in the unseen.
Always choose faith and let
things unfold the way they are
meant to. Not how you
planned them to.

Healing doesn't mean the pain
never existed. It means we
allowed our pain to turn into
beauty, our lessons to turn
into wisdom, and our
brokenness to turn into
wholeness. Everything you've
been through has shaped you
into the person you are today.
Today you walk over the
things you used to trip on.

To be vulnerable is to be
strong. You are not weak, you
are not broken, and no one
has the power to crush your
spirit. You may be wounded
but wounds heal and your
hardest battles will turn into
your greatest victories. Don't
give up on yourself because
the darkness you're in today
will lead you into the light.

The greatest pain of a wounded soul is the
pain of being in love with someone you can
never be with and grieving the loss of
someone who still lives.

N. Niami

ABOUT THE AUTHOR

N. Niami is an author, spiritual mentor, and speaker but above all, she is a woman of God and a believer. Christ alone defines the woman she is and her identity is built purely on Him. Her passion to help others has become her purpose in life and she is determined to empower those who have been hurt and heal the broken-hearted by sharing her personal journey and experiences. Coming from a place of brokenness herself she knows what it feels like to be in that dark place desperately waiting to see the light at the end of the tunnel. It wasn't until she refused to wait any longer and decided to become the light she needed instead. And from there on her mission to empower people around the world began. She is determined to be a living testimony to God's unfailing love, grace, and mercy. And she wants to assure you that the pain you've been feeling now can't compare to the joy that is coming.

For more information visit:
www.nniami.com

"Sometimes letting things go is an act of far greater power than defending or hanging on."

Eckhart Tolle

www.ingramcontent.com/pod-product-compliance
Lightning Source LLC
Chambersburg PA
CBHW032137020426
42334CB00016B/1199